Step-by-Step
Paperfolding

Clive Stevens

Heinemann
LIBRARY

www.heinemann.co.uk

Visit our website to find out more information about Heinemann Library books

To order:

 Phone 44 (0) 1865 888066

 Send a fax to 44 (0) 1865 314091

 Visit the Heinemann Bookshop at www.heinemann.co.uk to browse our catalogue and order online

Produced by Search Press Limited in Great Britain 2001.
First published by Heinemann Library, Halley Court, Jordan Hill, Oxford OX2 8EJ, a division of Reed Educational and Professional Publishing Ltd. Heinemann is a registered trademark of Reed Educational & Professional Publishing Limited.

OXFORD   MELBOURNE   AUCKLAND
JOHANNESBURG   BLANTYRE   GABORONE
IBADAN   PORTSMOUTH NH (USA)   CHICAGO

Text copyright © Clive Stevens 2001
Photographs by Search Press Studios
Photographs and design copyright © Search Press Limited 2001

Originated by Graphics '91 Pte Ltd., Singapore
Printed in Hong Kong

ISBN 0 43111 178 2 (paperback)
05 04 03 02 01
10 9 8 7 6 5 4 3 2 1

ISBN 0 43111 168 5 (hardback)
04 03
10 9 8 7 6 5 4 3 2

British Library Cataloguing in Publication Data

Stevens, Clive
Paperfolding. – (Step-by-Step)
1.Paper work – Juvenile literature
2.Origami – Juvenile literature
I.Title
736.9'8

Acknowledgements
The Publishers would like to thank the Bridgeman Art Library for permission to reproduce the photograph on pages 4-5.

Every effort has been made to contact copyright holders of any material reproduced in this book. Any omissions will be rectified in subsequent printings if notice is given to the Publisher.

To my daughter Angie, who I know will enjoy sharing all of the projects in this book with her young pupils.

Special thanks to G F Smith & Son London Ltd., 2 Leathermarket, Weston Street, London SE1 3ET for supplying the paper in this book. Many thanks are also due to everyone at Search Press who helped me with this book, especially Editorial Director Roz Dace and Editor Chantal Roser for their help and guidance, and Designer Tamsin Hayes for putting it all together.

• • • • • • • • • • • • • • • • • •

The Publishers would like to say a huge thank you to Joe Clarke, Tom Clarke, Natasha Nokes, Lloyd Perry, Gilly Armour, Caroline Armour and Christopher Armour.

Special thanks are also due to Southborough Primary School, Tunbridge Wells.

When this sign is used in the book, it means that adult supervision is needed.

REMEMBER!
Ask an adult to help you when you see this sign.

Contents

Introduction 4

Materials 6

Techniques 8

Pirate Hat 10

Glider Plane 12

Spinning Windmill 14

Twisted Pot 16

Bat Mobile 18

Pleated Picture Frame 20

Bird and Worm Card 22

Treasure Chest 24

Elephant Mask 26

Patterns 28

Index 32

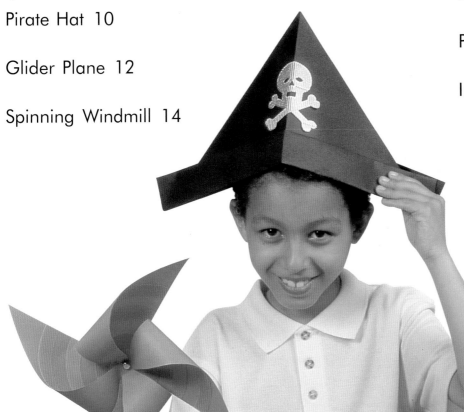

Introduction

Paperfolding is not only an ancient art, but it is one that requires very little equipment or space. As long as you have paper, a pair of scissors and some glue you can create a variety of wonderful sculptural shapes.

The art of paperfolding is thought to date back to the first or second century AD in China. The Japanese were practising this art by the sixth century and they called it origami (pronounced or-i-GA-me). The word is made up from 'ori', the Japanese word for folding, and 'kami', the word for paper.

In Japan, paper was scarce long ago, so only wealthy people could afford to do paperfolding. But as easier methods of papermaking were developed, paper became less expensive and paperfolding became a popular art for everyone.

The Japanese were not the only people folding paper. The Moors from North Africa were also practising this art. Their religion forbade the creation of representational figures, so their paperfolding took the form of geometric decorative designs, and they took their techniques with them when they invaded Spain during the eighth century. From there, paperfolding spread to South America, then to other parts of Europe as trade routes opened up, and later it spread to the United States. In Victorian England, it became a popular children's pastime. Paper hats, similar to the square hat worn by the carpenter in Lewis Carroll's *Alice Through the Looking Glass*, were made.

In this book you begin with basic scoring and folding techniques, then go on to enjoy making a pirate hat, a glider plane, an animal mask and many other exciting

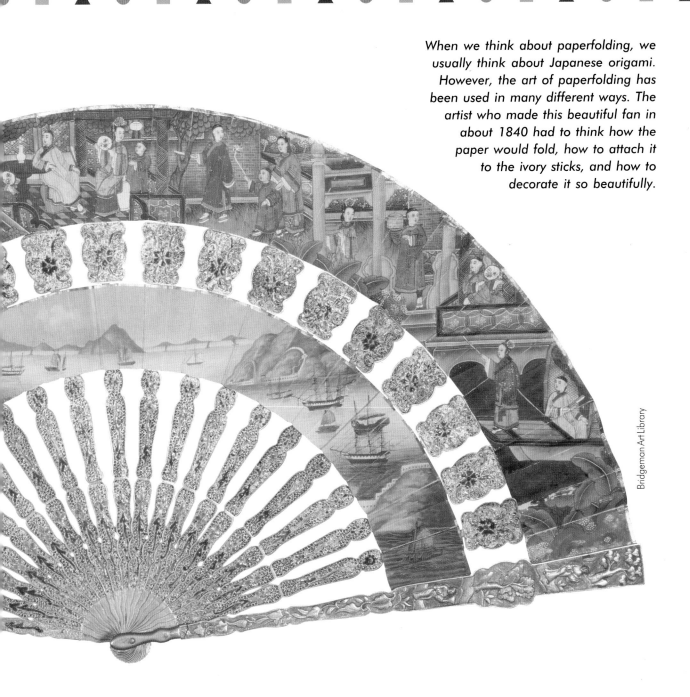

When we think about paperfolding, we usually think about Japanese origami. However, the art of paperfolding has been used in many different ways. The artist who made this beautiful fan in about 1840 had to think how the paper would fold, how to attach it to the ivory sticks, and how to decorate it so beautifully.

projects. You can also have fun designing and creating your own ideas. Be inventive by using different textured paper like thin corrugated card, brown wrapping paper, metallic and handmade paper. Or try using patterned paper such as gift wrap, wallpaper or pages from a magazine.

With paperfolding you can create wonderful greetings cards for your friends and family and design interesting gift wrap for a special present. So, have fun – and happy paperfolding!

Materials

The best thing about paperfolding is that it does not cost much to get started. You will not need all the materials shown on this page to begin, and you may already have some of them at home. Other items are easy to buy from local shops. In addition, there are some specific items needed for certain projects, such as cotton thread, a brass split pin, a paper clip, clear sticky tape and a coat hanger. You should check the list of materials carefully before you start each project.

All sorts of **card** and **paper** can be used for paperfolding. Thin, coloured card and paper are ideal, but so are single corrugated cardboard and metallic card.

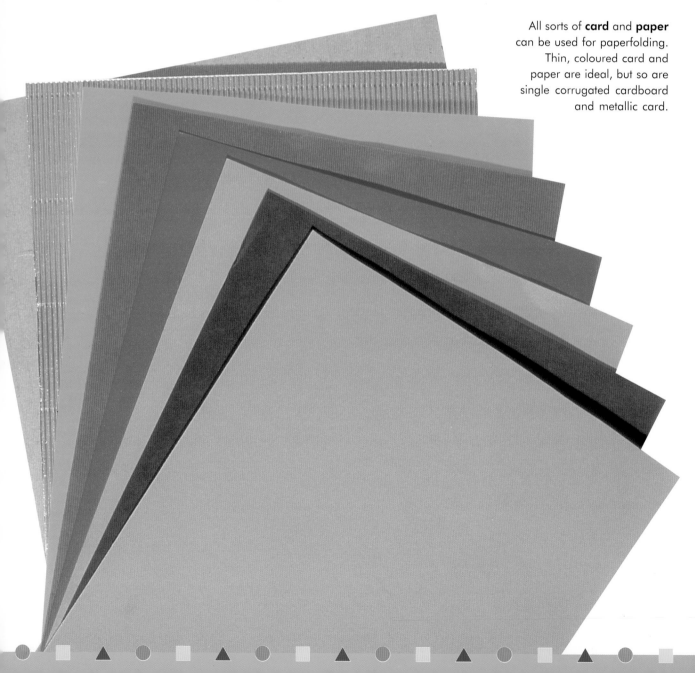

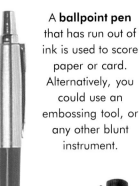

A **ballpoint pen** that has run out of ink is used to score paper or card. Alternatively, you could use an embossing tool, or any other blunt instrument.

Scissors are used to cut out card, paper and cardboard.

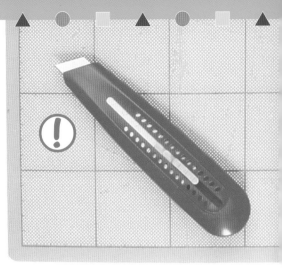

A **craft knife** is used to cut out intricate designs and to make small slits. Always ask an adult to do this for you as it is very sharp. A craft knife should always be used on a **cutting mat**.

A **black marker pen** is used to add detail to projects.

Strips of card are secured with a **stapler**.

PVA glue is used to stick surfaces together. Double-sided tape can be used instead of glue. It is more fiddly to use but it can prevent the paper and card from distorting.

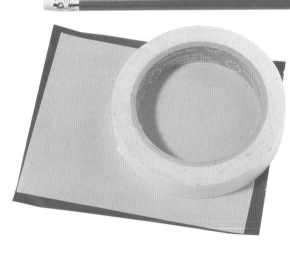

Tracing paper, **carbon paper** and a **pencil** are used when transferring designs. **Masking tape** should be used to hold the designs in place.

A **ruler** is used for measuring and for scoring straight lines.

Techniques

There are several basic paperfolding techniques. Freehand folding is simply folding paper without scoring or measuring the paper or card. To create intricate shapes it is helpful to score the paper or card first with a blunt instrument. Folding away from you makes a valley fold. Folding towards you makes a mountain fold. These are shown in the patterns as dots and dashes for valley folds, and dashes for mountain folds (see page 28).

Scoring straight lines

Place a ruler on the piece of card, where you want the line to be. Use the ruler as a guide and run an empty ballpoint pen along the edge to make an indent in the paper.

Scoring curves

Cut out a cardboard template of the shape you need. Run an empty ballpoint pen along the edge of the template to make an indent in the paper. Alternatively, you can score a curve freehand.

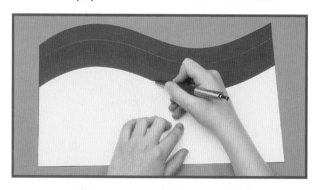

Hard-folding

Fold the card over along the line you have scored. To hard-fold, use the side of your finger-nail to make a neat fold along the scored line.

Soft-folding

Gently pinch along the scored line with your fingers. Repeat several times.

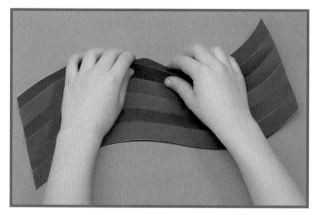

Making a template

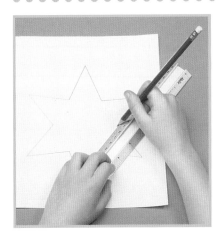

1 Place a piece of tracing paper over the pattern (see pages 28-31). Tape it down with small pieces of masking tape. Trace around the outline using a pencil. You can use a ruler if the pattern has straight lines. Remove the tape from the tracing paper.

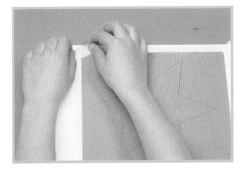

2 Place a piece of carbon paper face down on the surface you want to transfer the design on to. Place the tracing over the top then tape it in place.

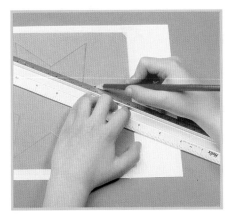

3 Trace around the outline with a pencil. Again, use a ruler for any straight lines.

4 Remove the tracing paper and carbon paper to reveal the transferred image.

Pirate Hat

This project only requires simple freehand folding and it is an age-old favourite. It was popular with Victorian children when they played at being pirates. The hat can be embellished by attaching cut-out designs, such as a skull and crossbones, or you could attach a feather if you want to make a Robin Hood hat.

YOU WILL NEED

Black paper
Thin metallic card
Tracing paper • Carbon paper
Masking tape • Pencil
Scissors • Craft knife
Cutting mat • PVA glue

1 Take a piece of black paper, the same size as an unfolded tabloid newspaper, and hard-fold it in half lengthways (see page 8).

2 Hard-fold the paper in half lengthways again.

3 Open up the last fold, then fold down the left-hand corner to the centre line. Repeat with the other corner.

4 Fold up the bottom edge nearest to you so that it meets the corners. Fold it up the same amount again. Turn the hat over and repeat on the other side.

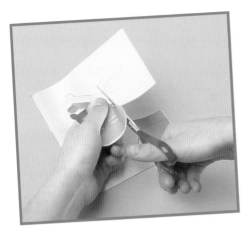

5

Trace the skull and crossbones pattern shown on page 31 on to metallic card (see page 9). Use scissors to cut out the main shape, and a craft knife to cut out the small shapes inside.

Craft knives are very sharp. Ask an adult to cut out the small shapes.

6

Fold the skull and crossbones in half lengthways, then glue it to the front of the hat, making sure that it lies over the central fold.

FURTHER IDEAS

Make a Robin Hood hat using different coloured paper. Using scissors, cut out a feather shape from card, score it down the middle then cut lots of slits in it.

Glider Plane

Your mother or father may have folded wonderful paper aeroplanes for you when you were younger. Well, here is one that you can easily make yourself, using freehand folding, soft-folding and one piece of coloured paper. The plane is decorated with cut-out thin coloured paper shapes which are glued on to the wings. You should never launch your finished plane towards other people.

YOU WILL NEED

Coloured paper
Scissors • PVA glue
Paper clip

1 Cut a piece of coloured paper approximately 25cm x 28cm (8½in x 11in). Score and soft-fold it in half lengthways (see page 8), then fold the top corners down to the centre line.

2 Fold each side in from the point, to meet the centre line.

3 Fold the tip back towards the middle, to the point where the sides meet to form the front of the plane.

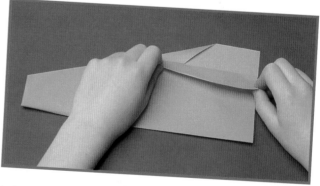

4 Fold the plane in half lengthways, then fold the top wing down about 1cm (½in). Turn the plane over and repeat on the other wing.

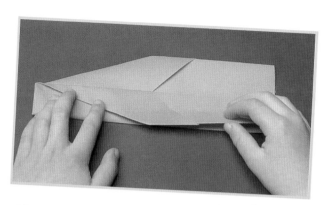

5 Fold the wing down again, from the top of the nose. Turn the plane over and repeat on the other wing.

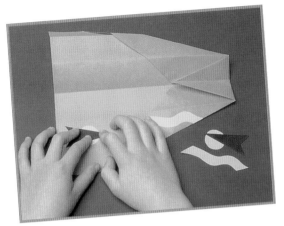

6 Flatten the plane out. Cut out your own decoration from coloured paper, then glue the shapes on to the wings.

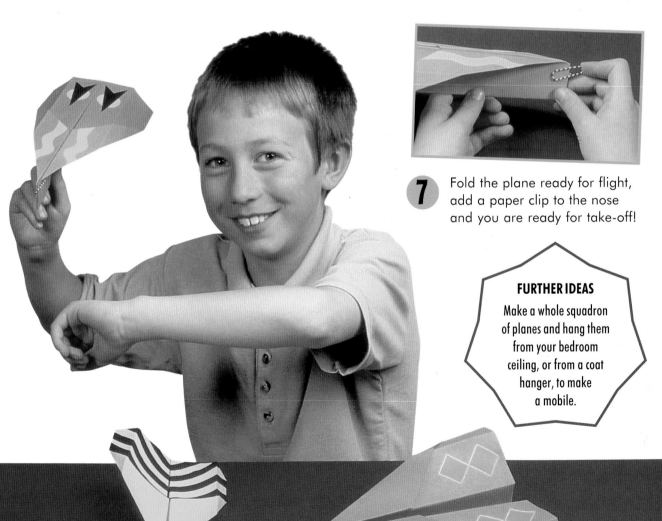

7 Fold the plane ready for flight, add a paper clip to the nose and you are ready for take-off!

FURTHER IDEAS

Make a whole squadron of planes and hang them from your bedroom ceiling, or from a coat hanger, to make a mobile.

Spinning Windmill

This simple design is made from brightly coloured thin card and decorated with different size dots in a contrasting colour. When the windmill spins, it forms wonderful coloured patterns. The handle is made by scoring lines along a length of thin card which is folded into a triangular stick.

YOU WILL NEED
Coloured paper
Thin card • Empty ballpoint pen
Ruler • Pencil • Scissors
PVA glue • Craft knife
Cutting mat
Brass split pin

1 Cut out a piece of coloured paper approximately 20cm (8in) square. Cut out some shapes from a different coloured paper and glue them on to the square.

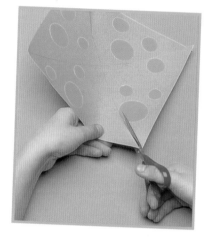

2 Use a ruler and pencil to draw two diagonal lines through the square to form a cross. Make a cut at each corner, exactly one third of the way along the pencil line.

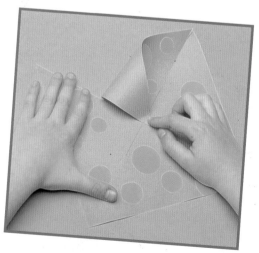

3 Pull one of the points down just past the centre and glue it in place. Hold it for a few moments until it is dry. Repeat with the other three points.

4 Cut out a rectangle of thin card, 4cm x 30cm (2in x 11¾in). Mark and score three lines 1cm (½in) apart. Fold along the lines, then form the card into a triangular stick. Glue in place and hold until dry.

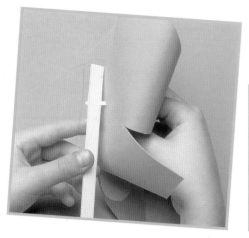

5 Use a craft knife to cut a very small slit in one end of the stick approximately 2cm (¾in) from the end. Make sure that it goes all the way through to the other side. Using scissors, cut a small hole in the centre of the windmill; push a split pin through it, then through the paper stick.

6 Carefully fold back the ends of the split pin, so that the windmill can turn.

FURTHER IDEAS
Make some colourful miniature windmills, tape them to cocktail sticks, then display them in a small vase or container.

Twisted Pot

With simple folds you can create some colourful crazy containers – and this ingenious little twisted pot is a wonderful example of cardboard engineering. You can decorate it with paper shapes, then fold and glue it to form a square box shape. With a simple twist it suddenly springs to life.

YOU WILL NEED

Thin coloured card
Coloured paper
Tracing paper • Carbon paper
Masking tape • Pencil
Empty ballpoint pen
Scissors • Ruler
PVA glue

1 Transfer the design shown on page 30 on to thin coloured card (see page 9). Cut out the rectangular shape. Score the card along the vertical and diagonal lines using an empty ballpoint pen and a ruler (see page 8).

2 Cut out shapes of your choice from coloured paper.

3 Use PVA glue to stick the paper shapes to the card. Leave to dry.

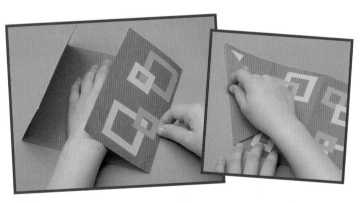

4 Hard-fold along all of the scored lines (see page 8). Turn the card pattern face-down and fold the vertical lines towards you. Turn the card over then fold the diagonal lines towards you.

5 Glue the flap to the other end to form an open-ended box. Hold between your finger and thumb for a few moments, then leave to dry thoroughly.

6 Flatten the box. Slowly push your thumbs together, then very gently twist your right hand towards you so that the pot springs into shape.

FURTHER IDEAS

You could make a set of small brightly coloured pots which can be used as egg cups for the whole family.

Bat Mobile

This fun mobile uses black and contrasting metallic card, so that when the stars and moon turn they reflect the light beautifully. The shapes are traced from the patterns, cut out and scored to create a three dimensional image. They are then suspended by thread on a coat hanger, but you could use an ordinary wooden stick or a wire rod.

YOU WILL NEED

Black and thin metallic card
Tracing paper • Carbon paper
Masking tape • Pencil
Scissors • Empty ballpoint pen
Ruler • Sharp pencil
Cotton thread • Clear sticky tape
Coat hanger

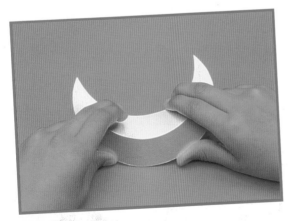

1 Transfer the bat, moon and star patterns from page 29 on to black and thin metallic card (see page 9). Cut out the shapes.

2 Score and then hard-fold the stars (see page 8) then open them up to form three-dimensional forms.

3 Score along the curved centre line of each moon and then soft-fold gently (see page 8).

4 Score each bat freehand, then soft-fold to give shape to the body and wings.

Thread lengths of cotton through the holes and secure on the underside with clear sticky tape.

Ask an adult to help you suspend your mobile from a suitable location.

Note You can adjust the way your mobile hangs by adding small pieces of removable adhesive to the pieces.

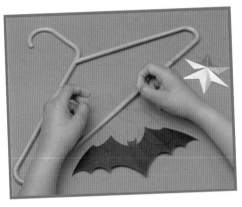

6 Tie the cotton on to a coat hanger to suspend the moon, stars and bats at different levels. Snip off any loose ends.

FURTHER IDEAS
You could cover the coat hanger with crepe paper. Decorate it with cut-out cloud shapes or shiny stars.

Pleated Picture Frame

Every artist needs a beautiful frame for a favourite picture or painting. It completes the effect and complements the image it surrounds. This project shows you how to create a simple pleated frame. The sides are glued on to a corrugated cardboard base and pleated corners are added in a contrasting colour.

YOU WILL NEED

Single corrugated cardboard
Thin coloured card
Scissors • Ruler
Empty ballpoint pen
Tracing paper • Carbon paper
Masking tape • Pencil
PVA glue

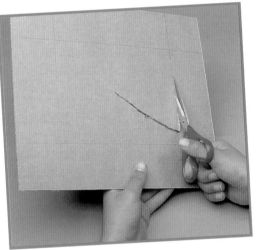

 Cut out a piece of corrugated cardboard 22cm x 25cm (8¾in x 10in). Draw a line 5cm (2in) in from each edge with a ruler and pencil. Cut out the centre to form a frame.

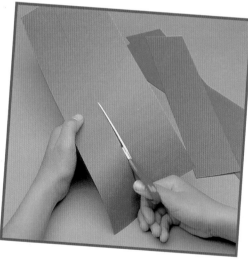

2 Cut out 2 strips of thin coloured card 6cm x 30cm (2¼in x 11¾in) and 2 strips 6cm x 27cm (2¼in x 10¾in).

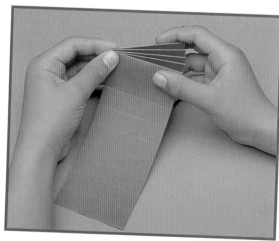

3 Mark lines 1.5cm (⅝in) apart all along each strip of coloured card. Pleat each strip by scoring and then hard-folding along the lines (see page 8).

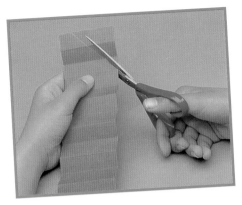

4

Open the pleated strips out. Mark a diagonal line from the third fold approximately 1cm (½in) in from the corner. Cut the corner off. Repeat on all ends of the coloured card strips.

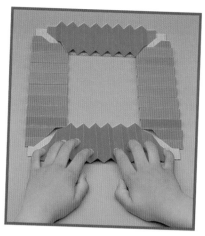

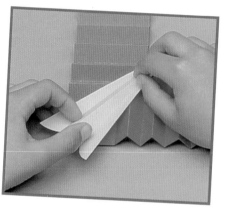

6

Transfer the pattern on page 29 on to coloured card four times (see page 9). Cut them out, score and pleat them, then glue them on to each corner to hide the joins.

5 Apply glue to the cardboard base, then position the pleated strips on top. Leave to dry.

FURTHER IDEAS
You can use circles or other shapes on the corners, and experiment with different sized pleats to create different effects.

Bird and Worm Card

It is always nice to receive and send homemade cards.
This pop-up card will amuse your family and friends and it
can be used for any occasion. It uses a simple fold to create
the pop-up action. The bird's head is transferred from the
pattern and glued to the card. A slit is then cut along the
beak and folded back. For the finishing touch a pink worm
is added to the inside of the beak.

YOU WILL NEED

Coloured paper
Thin card • Scissors
Tracing paper • Carbon paper
Masking tape • Pencil
PVA Glue

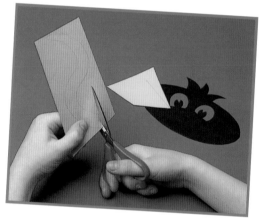

1 Transfer the bird and worm
patterns on page 29 on to
coloured paper (see page 9).
Cut out the shapes.

2 Cut out a piece of thin card
approximately 36cm x 26cm
(14¼in x 10¼in). Fold the card in half,
and then in half again.

3 Unfold the card once and lay it flat,
with the first fold at the top. Glue the
beak on to the bird, then glue the
bird on to the inside of the open card.

4 Open the
card up
completely.
Fold it inside
out and cut
a slit along
the line on
the beak.

5 Hard-fold the top of the beak up, and the bottom of the beak back (see page 8).

6 Re-fold the card and pull the beak up to open the mouth. Fold the worm over the bottom of the beak and glue it in place inside the mouth.

FURTHER IDEAS

You can adapt the patterns to make other animals. Try making a frog with a fly in its mouth. The worm can become the frog's tongue and you can use tracing paper to make the wings for the fly.

Treasure Chest

Everyone has a collection of different things that they treasure and want to keep safe or hidden away. It could be special pebbles, shiny beads or secret messages. This little treasure chest is just the thing to store them in. It is made to look like the real thing by using a black marker pen to add the bolt heads and a lock.

YOU WILL NEED

Thin coloured card
Metallic paper
Empty ballpoint pen
Black permanent marker pen
Ruler • Tracing paper
Carbon paper • Masking tape
Pencil • Scissors
PVA glue

1

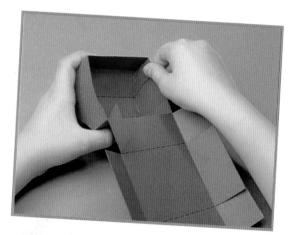

Transfer the basic chest pattern on page 28 on to thin coloured card (see page 9). Cut out the shape, then cut along the solid cut lines.

2 Score and hard-fold along all the dotted lines (see page 8).

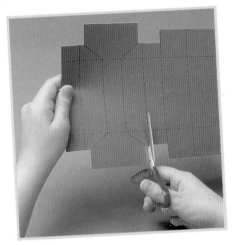

3 Glue the back of the angled tabs 1, 2, 3, 4 to the inside of the lid ends. Now glue tabs 5, 6, 7, 8 to the inside of the lid ends in the same way, to complete the lid

4 Glue the back of the corner tabs 9, 10, 11 and 12 to the inside of the base ends to form a box.

5 Transfer the lock design shown on page 28 on to metallic paper (see page 9). Cut out thin metallic paper strips and then glue the lock and strips on to the chest.

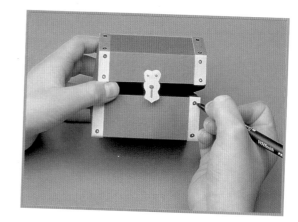

6 Use a black marker pen to add detailing to the lock, and make black circles along the metallic strips to represent bolt heads.

FURTHER IDEAS
Use metallic card and make a shiny treasure chest for your keepsakes, or decorate a coloured chest with interesting shapes.

Elephant Mask

Everyone loves masks. They are great fun to make and wear and they can transform you into something, or someone, completely different. This project is easy to do and it can be adapted if you want to create a different animal.

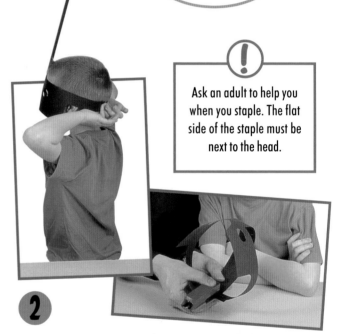

(!)

Ask an adult to help you when you staple. The flat side of the staple must be next to the head.

1 Cut out a piece of thin black card approximately 70cm x 50cm (27½in x 19¾in). Fold the card in half widthways, then align the marked edge of the basic mask pattern on page 30 along the fold. Transfer the pattern on to the card (see page 9), then cut out the shapes.

2 Open up the mask and fit the side tabs around your head. Hold them in position, remove the mask then staple the ends. Replace the mask on your head and take the front strip over the top of your head. Hold in position, remove and staple in place.

3 Transfer the face, ears and trunk patterns on pages 30 and 31 on to thin coloured card. Cut them out. Score along the fold lines of the trunk (see page 8) and then form it into pleats.

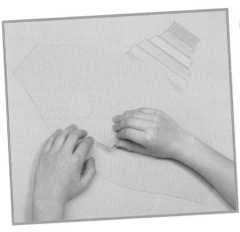

4 Use scissors to cut out the eye holes. Use a craft knife to cut a slit in the face where the trunk goes. Insert the trunk into the slit and tape in place.

Craft knives are sharp. Ask an adult to cut the slit in the trunk.

FURTHER IDEAS
You can adapt the pattern and use different coloured card to make a pig mask.

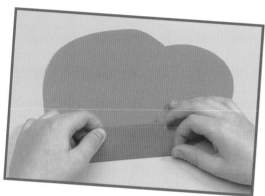

5 Fold the ears along the fold lines then ask an adult to staple them to the sides of the basic mask.

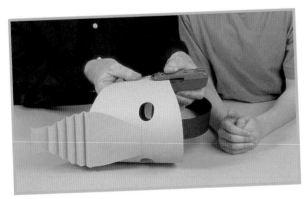

6 Ask an adult to attach the face to the basic mask with staples, making sure the eyes line up.

27

Patterns

Enlarge these patterns on a photocopier by 200%, then use them to make the templates for the projects (see page 9).

The patterns show two types of fold. Sometimes you need to fold the paper away from you. These folds are called valley folds. They are shown as dots and dashes. When you fold towards you, it's called a mountain fold. These folds are shown as dashes.

Get an adult to help you photocopy the patterns.

—·—·—·—·—·—·—·—·—·— *Valley fold – fold away from you*

------------------------------- *Mountain fold – fold towards you*

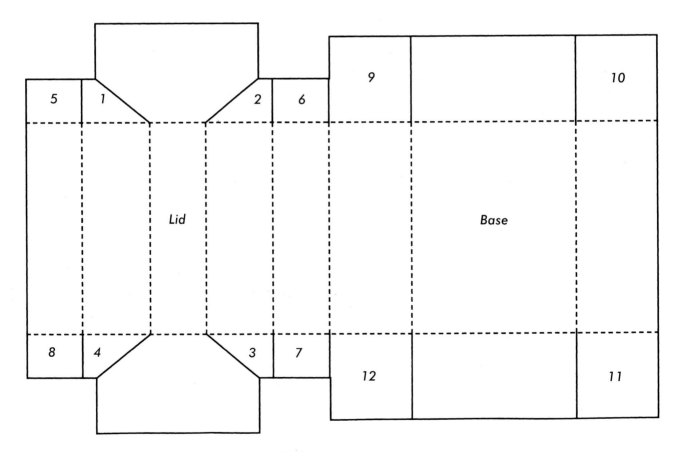

5 1 2 6 9 10

Lid Base

8 4 3 7 12 11

Patterns for the Treasure Chest featured on pages 24–25.

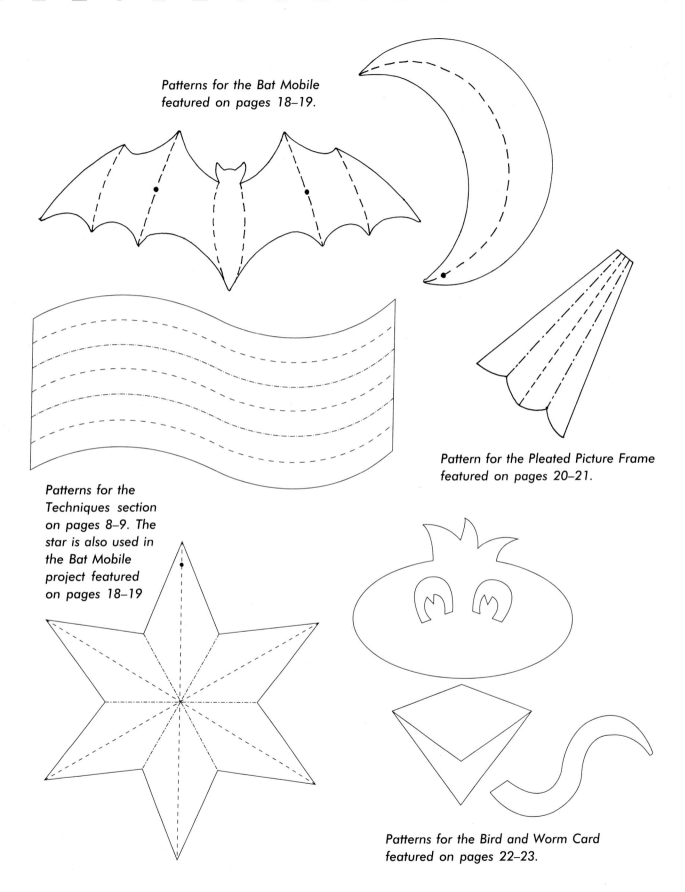

Patterns for the Bat Mobile
featured on pages 18–19.

Pattern for the Pleated Picture Frame
featured on pages 20–21.

Patterns for the
Techniques section
on pages 8–9. The
star is also used in
the Bat Mobile
project featured
on pages 18–19

Patterns for the Bird and Worm Card
featured on pages 22–23.

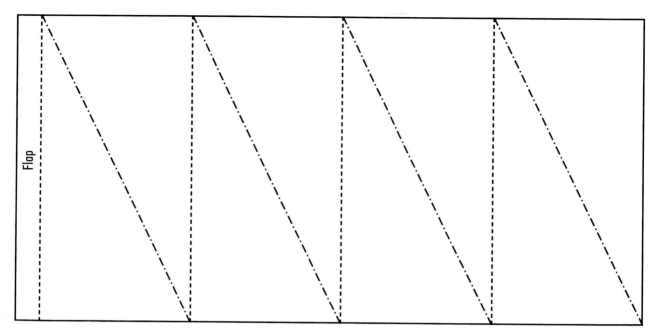

Pattern for the Twisted Pot featured on pages 16–17.

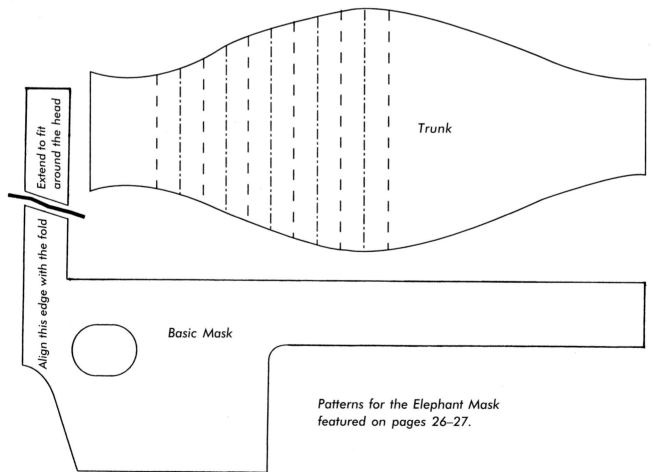

Flap

Extend to fit around the head

Align this edge with the fold

Trunk

Basic Mask

Patterns for the Elephant Mask featured on pages 26–27.

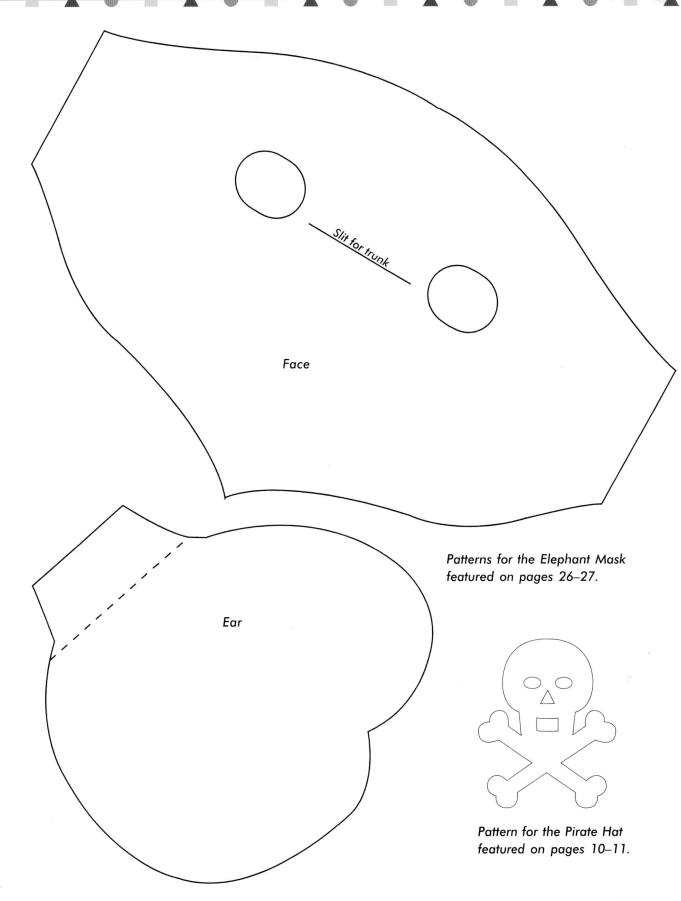

Slit for trunk

Face

Ear

Patterns for the Elephant Mask
featured on pages 26–27.

Pattern for the Pirate Hat
featured on pages 10–11.

Index

bats 18, 19, 29

carbon paper 7, 9, 10, 14, 18, 20, 22, 24, 26

card 5, 6, 7, 8, 14, 20, 21, 22–23, 24, 26, 29

cardboard 7, 21

chest 24–25, 28

coat hanger 6, 13, 18, 19

corrugated cardboard 6, 20

cotton thread 6, 18

craft knife 7, 10, 14, 15, 26, 27

curves 8, 18

cutting mat 7, 10, 14, 26

double-sided tape 7

fan 5

feather 10, 11

frame 20–21, 29

freehand folding 8, 10, 12

gift wrap 5

greetings cards 5

hard-folding 8, 10, 16, 18, 20, 23, 24

hats 4, 10–11, 31

mask 4, 26–27, 30, 31

metallic card 6, 10, 18

metallic paper 5, 24, 25

mobile 13, 18–19, 29

moon 18, 19

mountain fold 8, 28

origami 4, 5

paper clip 6, 12, 13

photocopier 28

pirates 10–11, 31

plane 4, 12–13

pot 16–17, 30

PVA glue 7, 10, 12, 14, 16, 20, 22, 24

Robin Hood 10, 11

scissors 4, 7, 10, 11, 12, 14, 15, 16, 18, 20, 22, 24, 26, 27

scoring 4, 7, 8, 11, 12, 14, 16, 18, 20, 21

skull and crossbones 10–11

soft-folding 8, 12, 18

split pin 6, 14, 15

stapler 7, 26

stars 18, 19

sticky tape 6, 18

template 8, 9, 28

tracing paper 7, 9, 10, 16, 18, 20, 22, 23, 24, 26

transferring 7, 16, 18, 21, 22, 24, 25, 26

valley fold 8, 28

Victorian 4, 9

windmill 14–15

Contents

Introduction to judo 6

The judo kit 8

In the dojo 10

Warming up 12

Breakfalls 14

Grips and throwing 16

Forward throws 18

Foot sweeps 20

Groundwork 22

Judo games 24

Competitions and rules 26

Judo terms 28

Further reading 29

Further information 29

Index 30

Introduction to judo

Judo is an exciting combat sport that started in Japan. The word *judo* means 'gentle way'. In judo the players do not hurt each other. They use a series of throwing and grappling techniques to put their opponents on the floor and hold them there. This is how they win contests.

Judo requires agility and balance. With these skills a smaller, lighter person can overcome a larger, more powerful person.

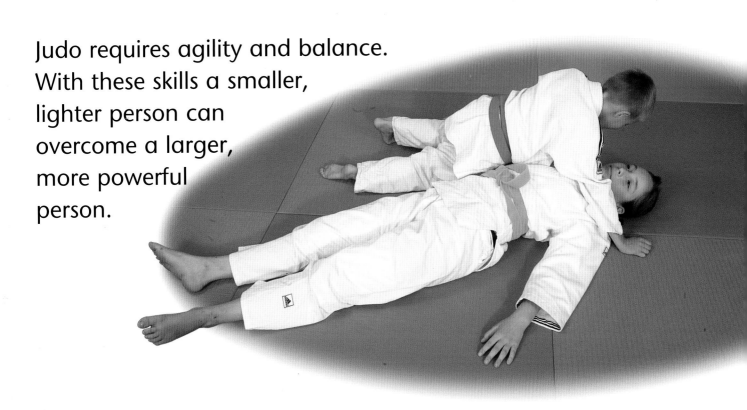

Judo terms

A judo player is called a *judoka*. An instructor is called a *sensei*. The room or hall where judo is taught is called the *dojo*. The floor of the dojo is covered by a thick, rubber mat called a *tatami*.

The judo kit

Judo is played wearing a judo outfit called a *judogi* or *gi*. This is a thick cotton jacket and trousers. A belt is tied around the waist. Girls can wear a white T-shirt under their jacket.

Tying the belt

Hold the belt in front of you and pass the two ends around your back, returning them to your front. Now pass the left end over the right, then pull it up behind both layers of the belt. Tie the free ends together right over left and pull them tight to make a knot.

Judo grades

You can tell what grade a judoka is by the colour of their belt. Beginners wear a white belt. Advanced players wear a black belt.

Junior players have 18 grades or *mons* which progress from a red belt through yellow, orange, green and blue to brown. At each colour stage you have to learn three things and for each one you get a bar on your belt.

When you have three bars, you can move on to the next belt colour.

In the dojo

Judo is a very respectful sport. Judokas and senseis must show respect to each other at all times.

Kneeling bow

At the beginning of a session all judokas make a kneeling bow or *za-rei* to their sensei. To do this, kneel on the floor and sit back on your calves. Keep your back straight and look forward. Now bend forward and slide your hands down your thighs onto the mat. Bow your head forward but not too close to the floor.

Standing bow

All judokas make a standing bow or *tachi-rei* to each other before and after a practice, and each time they change partners.

To do this, face your partner with your hands at your sides.

Bow your head and body forwards smoothly but not too far. Hold the position for a second then stand up straight.

Safety in the dojo

In judo no-one must wear anything that could hurt anyone.

- All jewellery, watches, earrings etc must be removed.
- Long hair must be tied back.
- Fingernails and toenails must be kept short.

NEVER do judo without a sensei present. ALWAYS do what your sensei instructs immediately.

Warming up

As with all sports, it is important to warm your body up and stretch your muscles before training. This will make you perform better and reduce the chances of you injuring yourself.

Exercises

1. Shoulder rolls: Stand up straight and roll your shoulders in a backwards direction. Do ten backward rolls then ten forward.

2. Sit ups: Lie on your back with your legs slightly bent. Without moving your legs, raise your upper body into a sitting position.

3. Squats: On the floor put your hands out in front of you and stretch your legs out behind. Jump forward into a squatting position. Jump backwards and forwards several times. This will strengthen the muscles in your legs.

4. Aerobic exercises: Get warm by doing some star jumps, windmill arms or running on the spot.

Breakfalls

One of the first things you learn in judo is how to fall safely.

There are three main types of breakfall: side breakfall, back breakfall and rolling breakfall. Which one you use depends on how you are thrown.

Side breakfall

Start from a squatting position. Put your right arm out and kick your right leg forwards. Roll to the right and slap the mat with your right arm. Keep your head off the mat.

Back breakfall

Crouch in a squatting position. Extend both arms in front of you. Tuck your head in and slowly fall backwards. Slap your arms flat on the floor. The harder you slap, the easier you will land. When you have become more confident, you can try it from standing up.

Rolling breakfall

From a standing position bend and put your left hand on the mat. Tuck your head in and roll over on your arm and shoulder. As you roll on to your back, slap the floor with your right hand.

Grips and throwing

Before you can throw you need to know how to grip your partner. In a basic right-hand grip, your right hand holds the front of your partner's gi and your left hand the sleeve. Your partner will also grip you like this.

When practising judo the judoka making the throw is called *tori* and the judoka being thrown is called *uke*.

The body drop

The body drop or *tai-otoshi* is a forward throw.
Tori uses a hand technique to unbalance uke.

As tori, first push
uke backwards. He
will resist and push
forwards. Use the
force of his push to
pull him forwards.
Then turn to the left
placing your right
leg across his
right ankle.

Make sure that your right
elbow is pushed
tightly under uke's
left armpit. As you
straighten your leg
you must lower
your body pulling
him off balance
and onto the mat.

Forward throws

Hip throw

The hip throw or *ogoshi* uses a powerful hip movement to lift the opponent up and over.

1. Start in the basic grip position and step in front of uke with your right foot.

2. Jump round moving your right hand around uke's back. Bend your knees and pull uke's hip against your back.

3. Straighten your legs and bend forward. Pull uke over your hips and back. Release your grip on uke's right arm so that he can fall to the ground without pulling you over too.

Throws using the arms and shoulders are called *seoinage* or shoulder throws.

One-handed shoulder throw

The one-handed shoulder throw or *ippon seoinage* is a popular throw and uses a quick turn and lift.

1. Step across with your right foot and turn your back on uke.

2. Bring your right arm under uke's right arm. Push uke's arm upwards whilst holding on to her sleeve with your left hand.

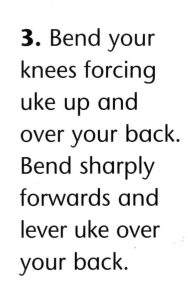

3. Bend your knees forcing uke up and over your back. Bend sharply forwards and lever uke over your back.

Foot sweeps

Throws that are used to trip your partner up with your foot are called foot sweeps.

Advanced foot sweep

In the advanced foot sweep or *deashi-barai* you force uke to take a step forwards and then sweep her foot away.

1. Push forward against uke and then step backwards to make her follow you.

2. As uke steps forward onto her right foot, sweep it away with the bottom of your left foot just as she is about to put her weight on it. At the same time pull down on uke's sleeve with your left hand.

3. Uke will lose balance and fall.

Fouls

Fouls in judo competition include: strikes to any part of the body; gouging, biting, scratching or spitting; hair pulling; bad language or loss of temper; holds where the fingers are inside the sleeve or trousers of the opponent (left) and any other unsporting behaviour. Any competitor receiving three fouls will be immediately disqualified.

Groundwork

When you and your partner have fallen or been thrown onto the mat you enter a stage called groundwork.

Groundwork is when players grapple on the mat, to get into a position where their partner cannot move. For beginners, groundwork is made up of hold-downs, which involve pinning the opponent down on the mat for up to 25 seconds.

Scarf hold

The easiest hold-down to learn is the scarf hold or *kesa-gatame.*

1. When uke has fallen at your side, quickly move and sit in the space between his right arm and his body. Hold his shoulders with both hands.

2. Wedge your hip tightly against uke's body as you put your right arm around his neck.

3. Spread your legs wide to keep stable. Lower your head and hold your opponent firmly.

Submission

When uke realizes he cannot get out of a hold-down he taps twice on the mat or on tori's body. When this happens, tori must release the hold immediately in order to avoid injury.

Judo games

Judo games are a good way for you to build up skills of balance and speed while having fun at the same time.

Sumo-style wrestling

Tie four or five judo belts together to make a ring. Two players wrestle each other inside the ring. They must try and unbalance their opponent, force them to step outside the ring or make them touch the floor with a hand or knee.

Surfing

This is a racing game. Line up several older players on their hands and knees. Smaller players stand on their backs. The pairs have to get to the other side of the mat as quickly as possible without the 'surfer' falling off. This is a good game to practise your balancing skills.

Drag racing

This is another pairs game that will strengthen your arms and legs! One player goes on their hands and knees while the other lies on their back and holds on to their partner's belt. The race is to the end of the mat.

Competitions and rules

Judo contests last for between three and five minutes depending on who is competing. The contest takes place on an 8-metre square mat with a red danger area marked around it and a green safety area outside that.

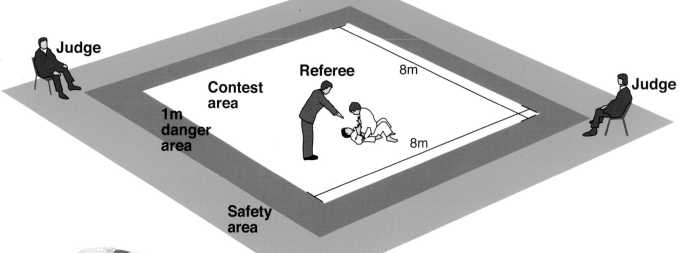

The aim of a judo contest is for a player to score 10 points. Ten points is called an *ippon*. There are two ways to score an ippon; one is to throw your opponent with force cleanly on their back, the other is to pin him down for 30 seconds.

If the throw is not quite perfect a *waza-ari* – a score of 7 points – may be awarded. Other scores for lesser throws and hold-downs are:
yuko, 5 points,
and *koka*, 3 points.

Rules

As judo is a physical combat sport, there are rules to make sure people do not get hurt.

• You cannot hold off an opponent by locking your arms out straight (below).

• You may not hold one side of your opponent's gi for more than 3 seconds without attacking them.

• You may not strike out at your opponent, kick him or push his face in any way.

Judo terms

deashi-barai advanced foot sweep

dojo the place where judo is practised

ippon a 10-point score that wins a contest

ippon seoinage one-armed shoulder throw

judo gentle way

judogi (gi) the suit worn when practising judo

judoka a judo player

kesa-gatame scarf hold

koka a 3-point score

mons junior grades

ogoshi hip throw

sensei teacher or master

seoinage shoulder throw

tachi-rei standing bow

tai-otoshi body drop

tatami judo mat

tori the person who performs a throw

uki the person who is thrown

wasa-ari a 7-point score

yuko a 5-point score

za-ei kneeling bow

Further reading

Judo in Action: Sports in Action, John Crossingham & Bobbie Kalman, Crabtree Publishing Company, 2006

Judo: A New Programme for White/Yellow Belt to Brown Belt, Hedda Sander & Bjorn Deling, Meyer & Meyer Sports Books, 2002

Judo for Juniors, Nicholas Soames, Ippon Books, 2001

Further information

British Judo Association
Suite B
Loughborough Tech Park
Epinal Way
Loughborough
LE11 3GE
Email: bja@britishjudo.org.uk
Website: www.britishjudo.org.uk

Australian Sports Commission
PO Box 176
Belconnen ACT 2616
Australia
Email: club.development@ausport.gov.au
Website: www.ausport.gov.au

Index

belt 8, 9, 24, 25
  bars on 9
  colour 9
  tying 8
body drop 17
breakfalls 14-15, 25

competitions 26-27
contests 6, 26-27

deashi-barai 20-21
dojo 7, 10, 11

exercises 12-13

foot sweeps 20-21
forward throws 18-19
fouls 21

gi 8, 16, 27
grades 9
groundwork 22-23

hand grip 16
hip throw 18

hold-downs 22-23, 26

instructor 7, 10
ippon 26

judo games 24-25
judogi See *gi*
judoka 7, 10, 11, 16

kesa-gatame 23
kit 8
kneeling bow 10
koka 27

mons 9

ogoshi 18
one-handed shoulder
  throw 19

rules 27

safety 11
scarf hold 23
sensei 7, 10, 11

seoinage 19
standing bow 11

tachi-rei 11
tai-otoshi 17
tatami 7
tori 16, 17, 23

uke 16, 17, 18, 19, 20,
  21, 23

warming up 12-13
waza-ari 27

yuko 27

za-rei 10